The Artist & Designer's
BOOK OF TIPS

12 Practical Tips & Spiritual Principles You Can Use Right Away

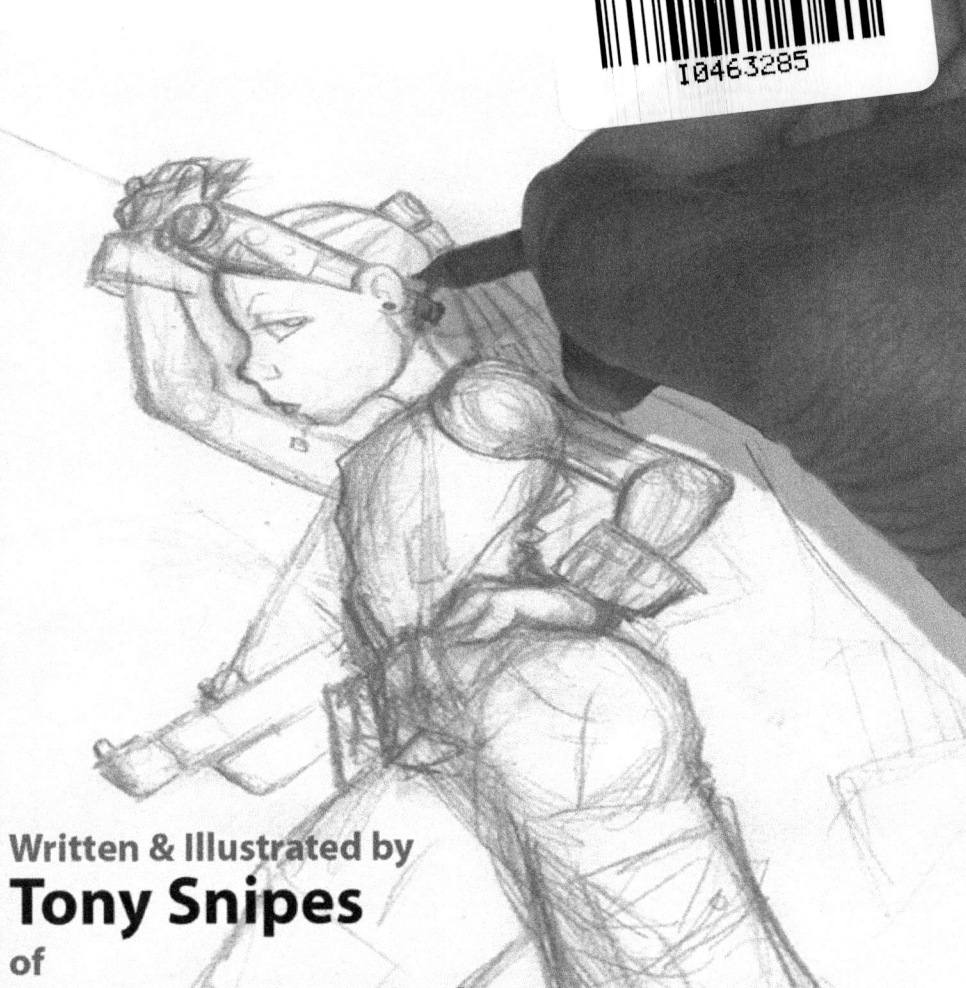

Written & Illustrated by
Tony Snipes
of
ArtLessonsFromGod.com

ArtLessonsFromGod.com Presents:

The Artist & Designer's Book of Tips
12 Practical Tips & Spiritual Principles You Can Use Right Away

Written & Illustrated By
Tony Snipes

Published By
Kreative Kingdom, Inc.
Inman, South Carolina

The Artist & Designer's Book of Tips- 12 Practical Tips & Spiritual Principles You Can Use Right Away.

ISBN 9781451589672

All Scripture quotations, unless otherwise indicated, are taken from The Holy Bible, King James Version.

To my beautiful wife, Monica:
Thank you so much for putting up with my late nights working on this book. Thank you also for believing me when I say that "it's all coming together."

I love you.
458!

CONTENTS

Acknowledgements

There are two people that I created this page for as a way to thank them for their attention to detail and their commitment to quality. I'd like to thank both Ms. Marian Smarr and Mrs. Gery Williams for taking the time to review and edit this book. They asked for nothing in exchange for the hours they spent reading and reviewing every sentence and every page in order to ensure that I had a professional product to deliver to my readers.

This book would not live up to the spirit of excellence it attempts to represent if it were not for the help of these two.

Chapter One:

YOUR ARTISTIC PURPOSE

How to Set Your Artistic Goals

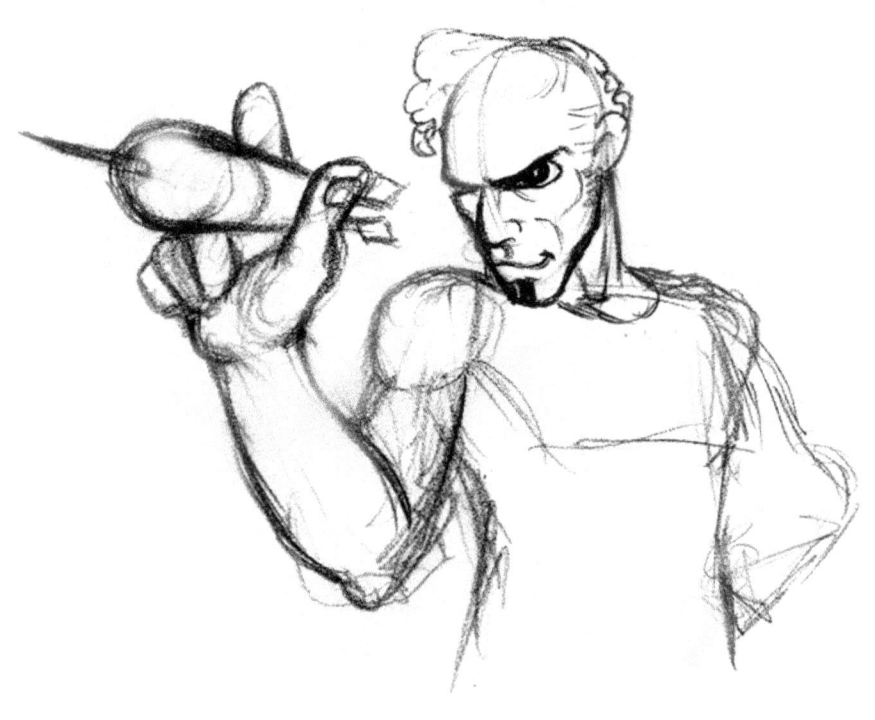

TIP NUMBER: 1

How to Set Your Artistic Goals

What did you accomplish artistically last year? Did you have a plan? What will you accomplish this month? Have a plan for it? God has a plan for you, your life and your creative ability. It's the reason why He gave you that ability in the first place; to accomplish something.

The cool thing about it is God does not want you to be in a guessing game with Him. On the contrary, He wants to reveal to you the steps to take to fulfill that artistic plan.

God tells us from the Bible:

"I will instruct you and teach you in the way you should go; I will counsel you and watch over you." Psalm 32:8

This scripture teaches that the Holy Spirit will be your practical guide. So, believe this even for the use of your artistic talents. Being of one mind with God, you walk out the plan from His perspective rather than from your limited point of view.

So where does an artist start? Let's start with the facts about the plan itself:

- A plan is a roadmap, predetermined for intentional progress.
- Success is achieved by a plan. Measuring the progress equates to measuring success.
- **Plans are flexible, but they MUST be present.**

Where to start?

Clearly identifying your goals is what helps to "spell out" the plan of action. God will reveal to you what He wants to accomplish through you using your creative gift. This is the "vision", the ability to see what God sees as the end result.

The bible says: "And the LORD answered me, and said, write the vision, and make it plain upon tables, that he may run that readeth it." Habakkuk 2:2

Revelation is when you see the same goal or vision God sees for your life and your creative ability. You recognize this when you get an idea you just can't let go, or you discover a concept you have so much passion for. Many times a creative job or favor you are asked to do is revealed as being an answer to someone's prayer. This in turn reveals how your gift fits into God's plan.

These things give clarity to the goal. What is God calling you to do with your creative gift?

Once the goal (or vision) is clearly identified, write down the practical steps required to make it happen.

Artists Becoming Able To Do What They Really Can't Do

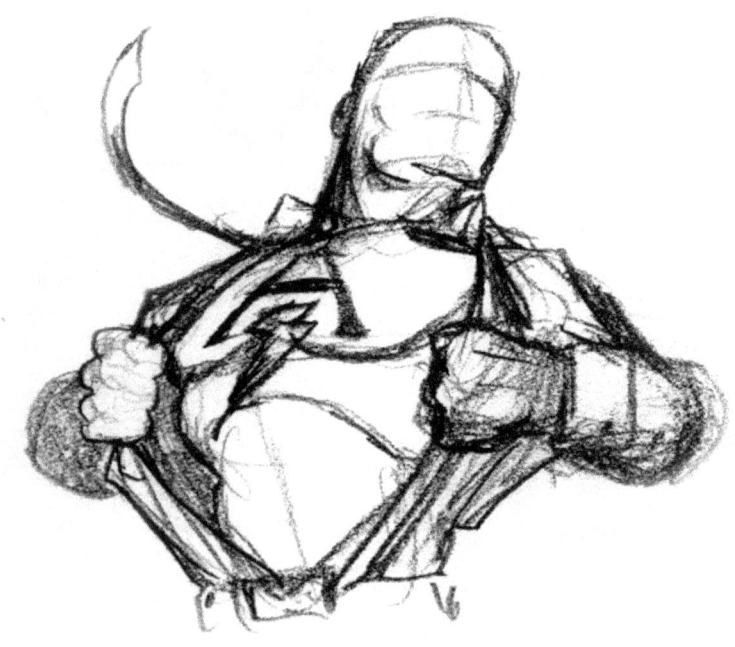

TIP NUMBER: 2

Artists Becoming Able to Do
What They Can't Really Do

Think about a time when you were given the chance to work on a creative project, commission, or gig that was a pretty big opportunity. Now picture it as one of those projects you knew would be almost too much of a challenge, be it skill, time, initial investment or whatever.

You recall the feeling you get when you know the opportunity is yours, but you also know it will cause you to really dig down deep to pull it off? Almost a feeling of inadequacy.

You are excited about having the opportunity; yet somehow you know that it's out of your league.

Welcome this feeling! It's an indicator that the stage is set for God to show up. An indicator that your creative talent is about to be used in a way proving only God can do it.

Being Able to Do What You Can't Do:

If you're an artist who has decided to have a relationship with God through Jesus Christ, you can be confident in the fact that God's power and ability is made perfect when the odds are stacked against you.

It may sound crazy, but you can actually welcome the feeling of incompetence. Now, this is not to say a lesser quality of craftsmanship is to be expected from or delivered by the Christian artist. Nor is it to say that training and practice are not needed. On the contrary, this may be the method of preparation leading to God working through you.

When you, the artist, are weak in human ability, you can be strong in divine ability:

God can accomplish more through your weakness than you could ever accomplish at full strength on your own. His Word teaches us the following:

"My grace is sufficient for you, for my power is made perfect in weakness.' Therefore I will boast all the more gladly about my weaknesses, so that Christ's power may rest on me. That is why, for Christ's sake, I delight in weaknesses, in insults, in hardships, in persecutions, in difficulties. For when I am weak, then I am strong." 2 Corinthians 12:9-10

So what steps do you take to make it happen?

First and foremost, you must have a relationship with Jesus Christ in order for this to work. This principle of God empowering you when you are at your weakest is not an earned quality, but an entitlement of the relationship.

Prayerfully acknowledge God's promises through scripture: I encourage artists to pray before embarking on the next project, especially the project that seems to be "out of your league." Study the scripture mentioned above and others like it. Pray for God's fulfillment of the scriptures (His Word) in your life. He promised it to you, that's why He wrote it down!

Take action and walk it out: When you sense that God has opened a door or presented an opportunity, take action, being confident that He will fulfill His Word. Be sure to learn what God directs you to learn. Practice what He presents to be practiced. Simply prepare yourself to be ready when He opens the door for a project that can only be accomplished under His ability through you.

5 Mistakes Many Artists Make

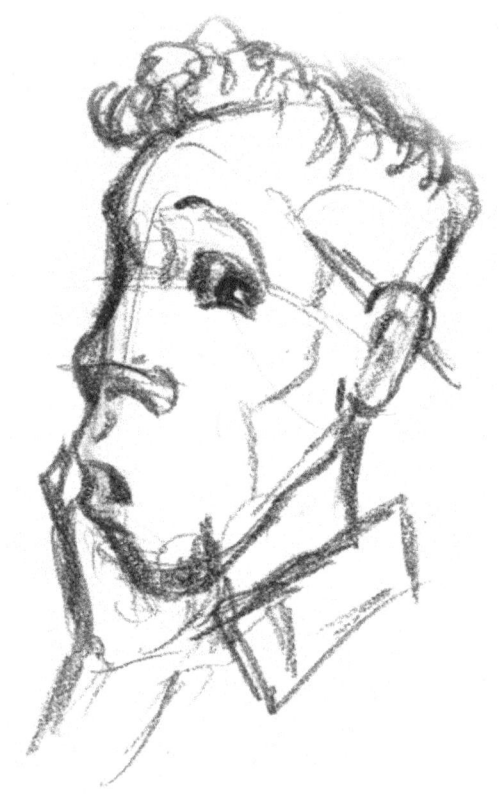

TIP NUMBER: 3

5 Mistakes Many Artists Make

Whether you are a Graphic Artist for a company; a freelance illustrator on your own; or a portrait artist working fulltime or on the side; you may have been (or even now still could be) guilty of one of the following mistakes many artists make:

1. Having no clear direction for yourself as an artist.

No matter what talent a person has, you must have some type of plan or goals for the use of that talent. The more talented and skilled you are, the more evident it is that your talent has a purpose. Many artists never take the time out to set a plan for themselves as artists. Part of the plan could be taking a class to improve your skills, or getting a certain amount of paid projects per month. The point is, set a plan and then work that plan.

A quick and easy solution: Get a journal, a notebook, or just a simple sheet of paper and write down the following:

Where have you been so far as an artist or designer?

Where do you think you're going (or would like to go or accomplish)?

How do you get there (taking classes, scheduling the creation of more work, join an arts group, etc.)?

2. Not having a web presence to show your work.

It's a shame that many artists strike up conversations with people interested in their work, yet they can't send this person anywhere on the web to view their portfolio. What's worst is that many of these same artists use the internet everyday. In this day and age, the person who gets the client's attention first is the artist that has an internet portfolio.

A quick and easy solution: Start with a free and easy-to-set-up blogging site. This can serve not only as a portfolio, but also as a way to communicate with current or prospective customers. I recommend Wordpress.com because of its ease in using it. This can be done right now as you take time to connect with other services or a web designer.

3. Not clearly identifying your audience.

Many business people make this mistake quite often. When you invest any amount of money to advertise or market yourself as an artist, you must be sure you know who is MOST LIKELY to do business with you. What is the average age? What is their average income? What do they like about your work, etc? The answers to these and a few other questions will allow you to target your marketing strategy to those most likely to respond.

A quick and easy solution: Ask yourself the following questions: Out of the last 10 customers who did business with you, how many were male/female? How many were local? How many from out of state? How many were 25-35 years old? How many were over 40, etc.? This should give you a very good idea of your TRUE target audience.

4. Not following up with people who've expressed interest in your work.

An artist who sells their work or services is a business person. Responding to an email or a phone call just makes good business sense.

A quick and easy solution: Make it a common practice to gather the email address of every customer who does business with you. Give them something in exchange for it (a discount or some other incentive).

Periodically send out special offers or event information. Use this tool carefully so that you will not be seen as a "stalker"!

5. Not keeping in contact with former clients.

Who else is more likely to buy your work now than someone who has already bought from you.

A quick and easy solution: The solution in number 4 above can be applied to this issue as well.

8 Ways to Get New Ideas

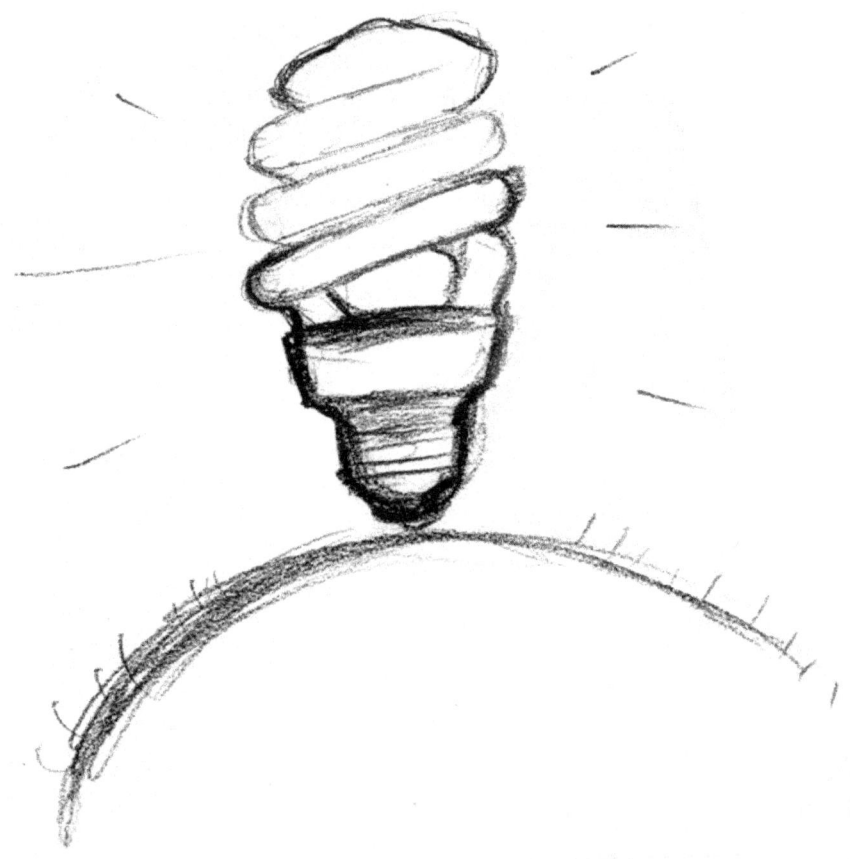

TIP NUMBER: 4

8 Ways to Get New Ideas

Every artist and designer is constantly looking for new ideas. Whether you are brainstorming on a new painting or looking for concepts to communicate a graphic design project, the search for new ideas is always on.

Here are 8 proven methods to get new ideas:

1. Take a walk: A simple but effective way to shut out the noise of any busy day and to tune in on concepts and ideas. I've taken time out of many lunch breaks in the busy corporate world to go outside, take a walk down the street, or a simple lap around the parking lot in order to "tune in".

2. Keep a journal/sketchbook: Make it a part of your lifestyle to keep a journal with you whether at work, home or in the car. This serves as a tool to write ideas and notions down when they hit you. The action of going back and looking at previous ideas that have yet to come to life will provide new ideas for the here and now. A sketchbook just adds another dimension to the capturing of ideas on paper since it allows you to illustrate what you see with your mind's eye.

3. Take a drive: A day trip creates the perfect environment for brainstorming on wheels. You can get ideas from time alone with your thoughts, or even create the environment for brainstorming by playing podcasts of speakers that speak on your subject of interest.

4. Take a shower: Notice how there is a trend of shutting out the noise of the outside world to finally gather your thoughts. A daily shower can create the proper venue to focus and allow concepts to come to mind.

5. Read a book: The action of reading a book is the earliest form of "downloading" ideas. Consider a book the brainstorm of another person whose thoughts have been captured for your benefit. There are many books available on art and design that will inspire you and get your ideas flowing.

6. ~~Talk~~ Listen to others: I crossed out "Talk" because the ability to speak rather than listening has probably lead to the drowning out of many great ideas. Listening to other artists, designers or other person's experiences always spark ideas. Those who have teachers are in a perfect position to benefit from this. Those who are currently not in a teacher-student relationship, seek out a mentor. You'd be surprised at the willingness and passion to help.

7. Put a new twist on an existing idea: Look around you and determine what creative expression can be done in a new and unique way.

8. Pray and watch: Dr. Henry Blackaby, co-author of the "Experiencing God" series points out that Jesus always said He knew what service He was to take on next because He would see the Father already involved. What this means to you is as you pray and ask God for ideas, be prepared as He opens doors. You will begin to see in some cases where ideas come to you.

Can You Lose Your Talent? 4 Ways To Revive It

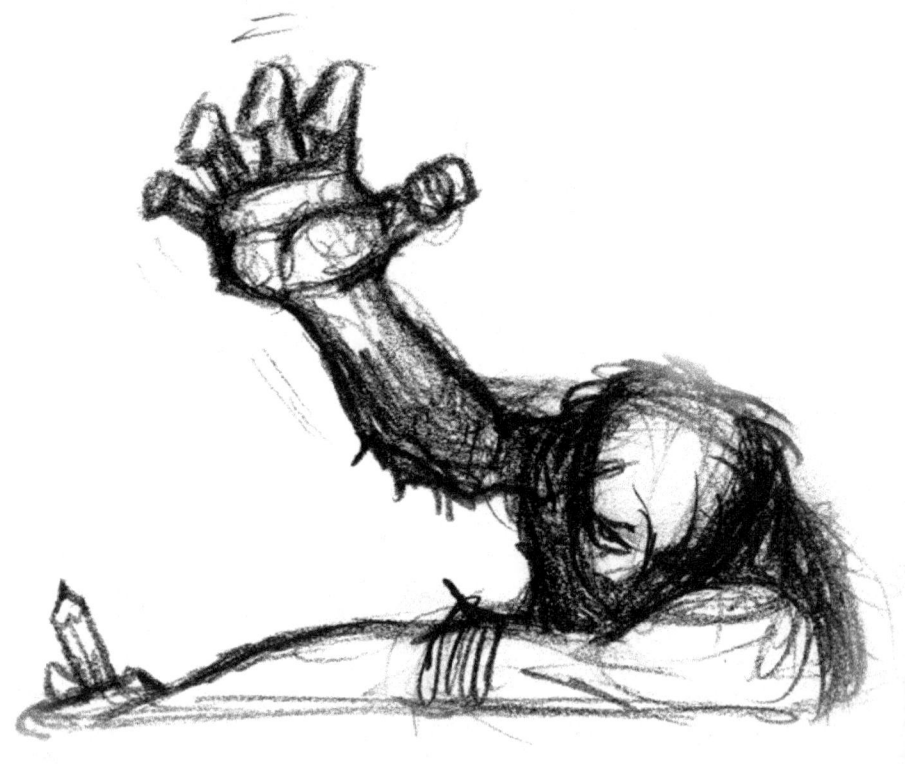

TIP NUMBER: 5

Can You Lose Your Talent? 4 Ways To Revive It

I've spoken with many individuals who, once they discover that I'm an artist, share the fact that they "used to be" an artist or "used to draw" as well.

Many of these individuals sound (understandably) disappointed as they seem to almost confess they once had this great gift, but no longer possess it. Usually, time and busy lifestyles are what led these "former" artists toward ceasing to operate in their God-given talent.

However, I don't believe they've seen their last sketchpad or paintbrush; and if they so desire, they can make a creative comeback.

The bible teaches us:

"For God's gifts and His call are irrevocable. (He never withdraws them once they are given, and He does not change His mind about those to whom He gives His grace or to whom He sends His call)." Romans 11:29 (Amplified Bible)

This tells you that God does not change His mind about the gift He's placed in you. Yes, it may have become rusty or even dormant having been put on the back burner, but that gift is still there...somewhere!

4 Ways to Revive Your "Lost" Talent:

1. Acknowledge your gift and the fact that although buried, it is still there. Although the skill may be rusty, it still can be revived.

2. Reflect on works you've done in the past. If possible, pull out old works as a demonstration of what you are capable of. This should serve as motivation and a testament to the skill you formerly put to work.

3. Practice, practice, practice. Start small and simple, yet consistent. Grab a sketchpad and sketch daily or keep a journal and sketch inspirations as they come to mind.

4. Set Goals determining what creative accomplishments you'd like to pursue. My personal goal was to do a certain number of digital paintings over a period of time. This allows intentional progress. The goals can be simple and flexible, but most of all they must be **present.**

Chapter Two:

GROWING INCOME WITH YOUR ART

3 New Ways To Make Extra Money With Your Art

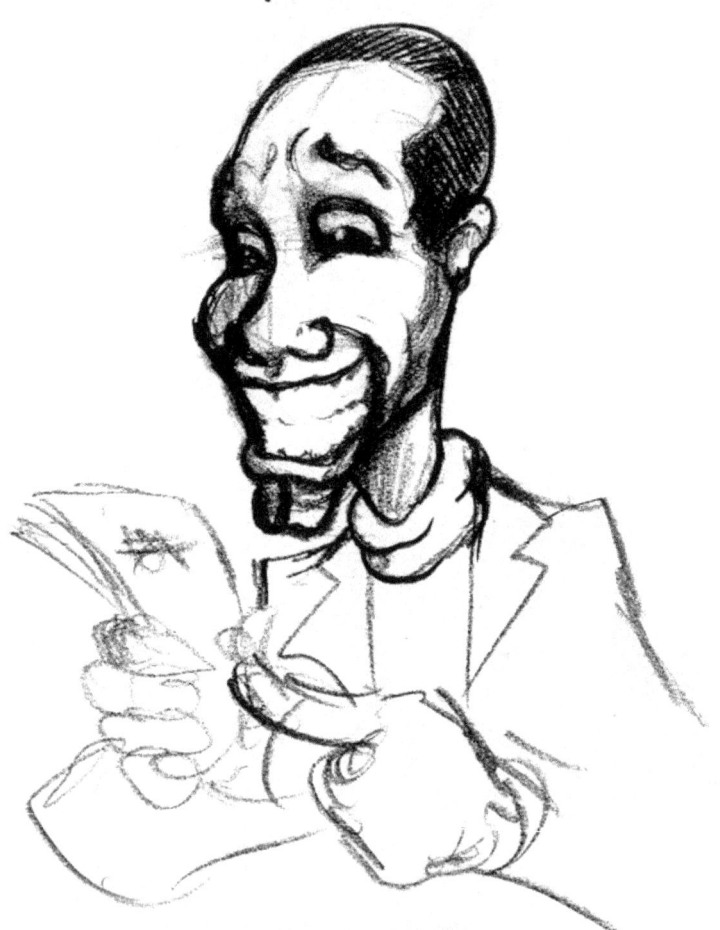

TIP NUMBER: 6

3 New Ways to Make Extra Money with your Art

To counter all the discussion about the challenges with the American economy, now is a good time to take a look at the talent you've been given in order to create a little (or a lot) of extra income.

Here are 3 new methods you can consider:

1. Custom Designs on Sneakers: You can now create your own designs on sneakers to sell to others or create logos or designs for someone else (individuals or businesses small or large). Go to this site to see how easy it is: http://www.zazzle.com/custom/shoes

2. Custom Designs on Travel Mugs: Not as expensive as their Sneaker option, Zazzle.com also has Travel Mugs that you can create and sell with your own custom designs or that you can design for others. Check it out here: http://www.zazzle.com/custom/mugs/travel

3. Custom Designs on Cell Phones and Computer Stuff: Help others customize their cell phones, laptops and other devices with SkinIt.com by HP: http://hp.skinit.com/

Remember, God has given you the strength and ability to use your gift to help others as well as earn an income: "…remember that the LORD your God gives you the strength to make a living. That's how He keeps the promise He made to your ancestors."
Deuteronomy 8:18 (Contemporary English Version)

16 Ways Artists & Designers Can Make Money In A Down Economy

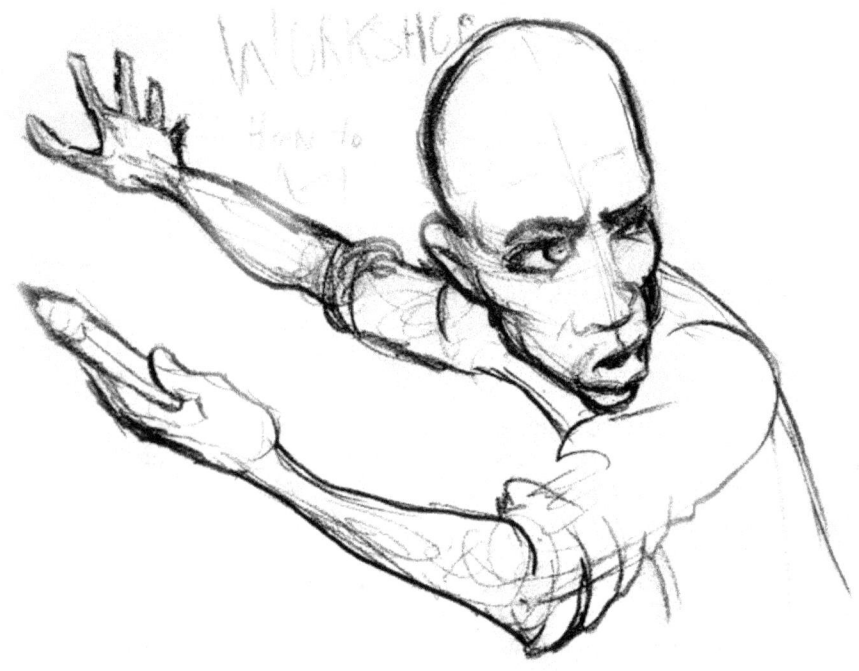

TIP NUMBER: 7

16 Ways Artists & Designers Can Make Money in a Down Economy

The upside about the state of the current economy is that it forces you as an artist or designer to tap into your God-given talent, creativity, and ability then use it to either help make ends meet or to earn a living all together.

God's Word says "The blessing of the Lord brings wealth, and he adds no trouble to it." Proverbs 10:22 (New International Version)

Here are 16 ways artists and designers can make money using their creative talent and abilities:

Classic "Old School" ideas that never fade:

1. Caricatures at kids' parties: Charge parents by the hour for this fun addition to their child's party. **EXPAND IT:** Rather than you seeking out parents on your own, partner with a kid's party venue (e.g. Chuck E. Cheeses, etc) and let the owner pay you per party.

2. Caricatures for HR department's: Human Resources departments always look for special perks for their employees, and with layoffs and bad news hanging over the head of their staff, they need a fun morale builder now more than ever.

3. Start a drawing class like Life Drawing.

4. Start a "Gamer Drawing Class" teaching others how to create dynamic character types found in video games. **EXPAND IT:** Rather than you seeking out patrons on your own, partner with a computer game store or gaming arcade and let the owner pay you per event as an attraction.

5. Have an "Artists Tag Sale" with multiple artists selling their old studies and similar works.

6. Speak, Speak, Speak! Give an artist's talk or presentation for an honorarium.

Customize gift ideas for those seeking "something different" since money is tight:

7. Do portraits from photos or in person

8. Pet Portraits from photos. EXPAND IT: Rather than you seeking out pet lovers on your own, partner with a pet store and let the owner pay you per event as an attraction.

9. Do portraits of homes for the homeowner
EXPAND IT: Rather than you seeking out homeowners on your own, partner with a real estate agent or broker letting them give the house portrait as a gift to the new homeowner as a thank you for doing business with them.

10. Create custom greeting cards

11. Make posters for local bands

12. Design t-shirts or other items (see Cafepress.com, Zazzle.com and Threadless.com)

"New School" ideas for the "Mid-to-High Tech" Artist or Designer:

13. Retouch old photos using Photoshop.

14. Create custom backgrounds for Twitter users:
Here's an example of a fellow artist who is already doing a great job with it: http://killertweets.com/

15. Create customized "skins" for gadgets such as cell phones, laptops, desktops, etc: Check out a site like Gelaskins.com for ideas. **EXPAND IT:** Partner with a cell phone store or computer store. You designing these onsite (or off) would be an extra attraction that they could use during these challenging times.

16. Create customized framed Montages using Photoshop: Most artists skilled in Photoshop could do this on their own, but here is a site that works with artists almost like a franchise for an montage business: http://newphotoworks.com/workfromhome.html

Chapter Three:

HEARING FROM GOD ABOUT YOUR TALENT

Artists Taking the Mystery Out of Hearing From God

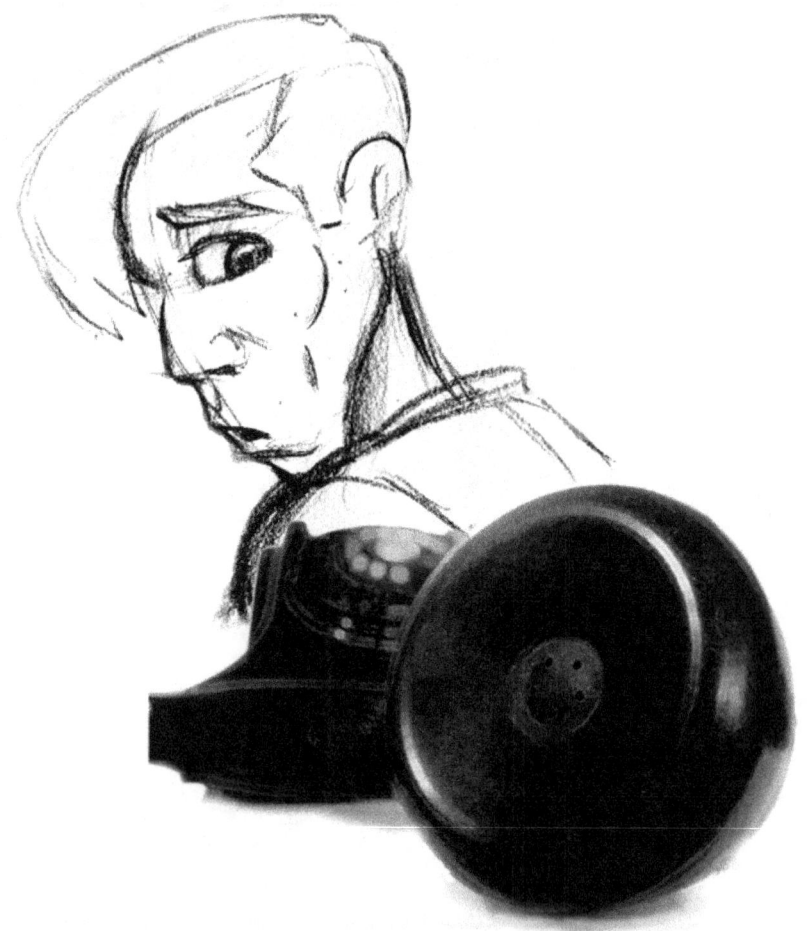

TIP NUMBER: 8

Artists Taking the Mystery Out of Hearing from God

Many of my readers and subscribers to my blog have shared that one of the key things you need is insight on how to hear from God, especially concerning the purpose and use of their creative talent.

With that said, I initially thought that writing this would be too basic, too simple. But honestly, it's usually the simple answers that we forsake, looking for some "deep" mysterious revelation.

On that note, here are 3 practices that will take the mystery out of hearing from God about your talent and everything else in your life: (You'll see that I used two very contemporary translations to make the meaning as basic and as simple as possible.)

1. Secrets are revealed simply by PRAYING: God talks to us when we talk to Him. He'll reveal secrets that we could never discover on our own:

"Ask me, and I will tell you things that you don't know and can't find out." Jeremiah 33:3 (Contemporary English Version)

2. See where you're going simply by READING: Much of what God wants to say to us is so important that He wrote it down!

"By your words I can see where I'm going; they throw a beam of light on my dark path." Psalm 119:105 (The Message)

3. DON'T SKIP CHURCH! It's so easy to be guilty of this one! God speaks to us through the believers He's placed in our lives to teach, coach, and motivate us:

"Some people have gotten out of the habit of meeting for worship, but we must not do that. We should keep on encouraging each other, especially since you know that the day of the Lord's coming is getting closer." Hebrews 10:25 (Contemporary English Version)

So, the initial answer to the question on "how to hear from God" lies with these SIMPLE questions:
• Do you have a daily prayer life?
• Are you reading and studying the bible daily?
• Are you a member of a church where a proper relationship in Christ is being taught and encouraged?

3 Ways Artists & Designers Hear from God

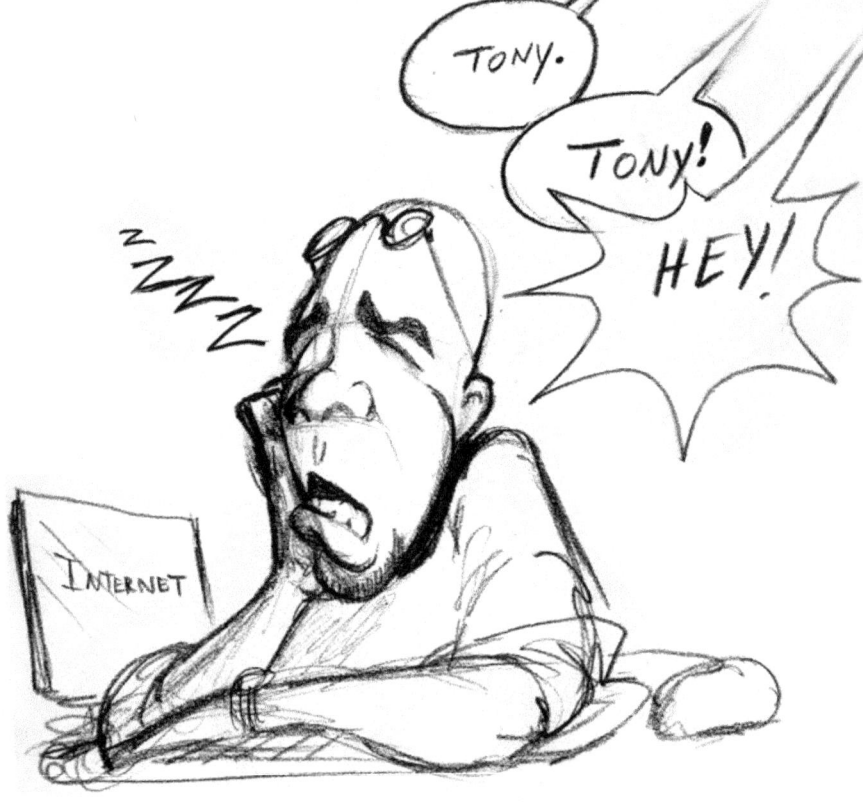

TIP NUMBER: 9

3 Ways Artists & Designers Hear from God

How do you hear from God concerning your creative talent?

How do you hear from God concerning ANYTHING for that matter?

There is no quick and easy formula, but the bible does give us confidence that God surely speaks to, guides, and directs His artists.

I believe the key principle here is that God speaks to us all the time, we just need to:

1. Be in the place where God is speaking in order to hear Him.

2. Get rid of the "noise" that tries to drown out the sound of His voice.

3. Refrain from silencing the voice of God when it conflicts with our own "voice".

Being "where God is speaking" means to be in the presence of God. This can be anywhere when you direct your mind and spirit toward God. That means in church, in fellowship with other believers, and especially in your own personal **quiet time** communing with God. You can liken this time to a briefing or meeting that God and you hold. The thing is, many times God is waiting to meet with you, but YOU don't show up to hear from Him.

You as an artist or designer can be encouraged by

Bezaleel, an artist from the book of Exodus:

"And Moses said unto the children of Israel, See, the LORD hath called by name Bezaleel the son of Uri, the son of Hur, of the tribe of Judah…" Exodus 35:30

God chose Bezaleel to use his talent to help create the ark of the covenant and the tabernacle where God met with the Hebrew people. Bezaleel's name means "In the shadow of El" or "In the shadow of God". This leads us to believe that "Bez" was an artist that spent time in God's presence.

The "noise" of day-to-day life can drown out the voice of God. Jesus was surrounded by people almost everyday, yet He dedicated time to step away from the crowds and spend quality time alone with God:

"And in the morning, rising up a great while before day, He went out, and departed into a solitary place, and there prayed." Mark 1:35

The voices of 24 hour TV, radio, cell phones, etc. keeps us accustomed to background noise. It is even more of a challenge to sit down in the quiet and read due to our fast growing multi-media culture. Jesus set the example for us by stealing away to commune with the Father, as He received direction from the Father.

Lastly, refrain from silencing the voice of God when it conflicts with your own "voice". Sometimes God has already spoken to you on many topics. What if His direction to you is the same thing that you'd rather not do? Many times when this happens, we convince ourselves that this wasn't God's voice, but our own. What you need to do is to condition yourself to be in a position of Neutrality. This means that you will be able to accept whatever God decides no matter how important your personal preference may be.

ArtLessonsFromGod.com

5 Steps Toward Artists Knowing and Completing The Will of God

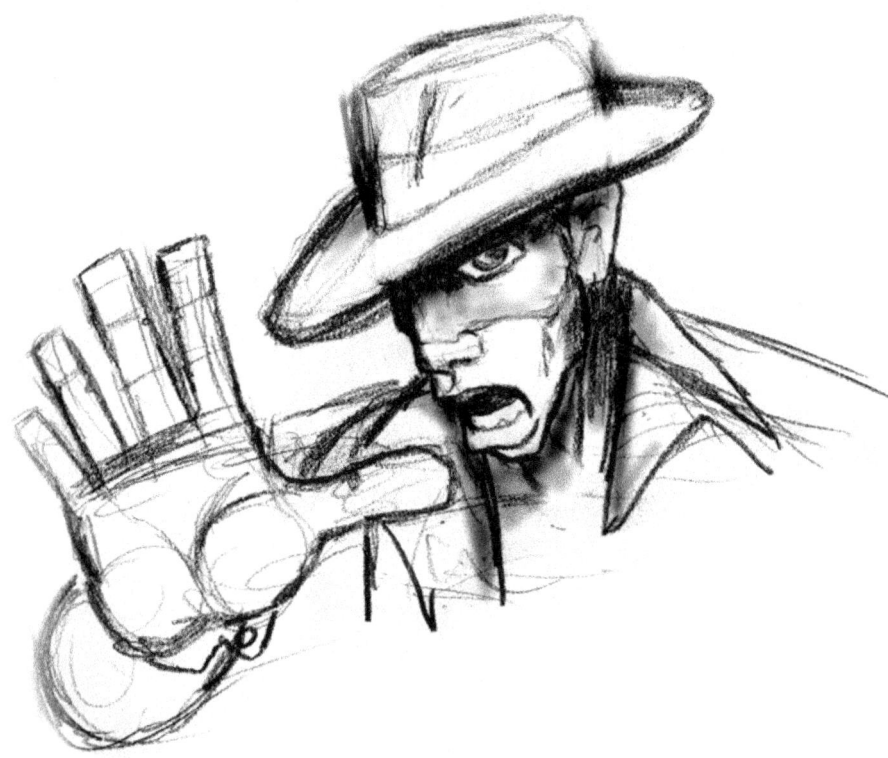

TIP NUMBER: 10

5 Steps Toward Artists Knowing and Completing the Will of God

This is a basic and simple method of knowing how to move ahead with a God–given assignment:

1. Ask yourself: "What is the last artistic endeavor that I know for sure, without a doubt, that God directed me to complete?"

This does not have to be something that's super deep or mysterious. It usually is that idea you can't get rid of, that thing you keep putting off, that painting you still haven't painted, the website portfolio you STILL haven't launched, etc.

2. After identifying something you KNOW God directed you to complete, ask yourself: "Have I completed it yet?"

If not, that's a good place to start. It's always wise to complete the last thing you know God directed you to do before expecting Him to reveal the next project.

This may be something you have placed on the back burner or you may have neglected it because it seemed small. Just remember: a small God-given idea will have much more Kingdom value than you spinning your wheels trying to launch a seemingly "good" idea.

You've now identified a few things you believe God has directed you to accomplish as an artist or designer. Now, the best part! How to take Action:

3. Write it down TODAY:

Grab a notepad, journal, or something you know you can find easily to refer back to.

Write down 3 to 5 key ideas, projects or goals you KNOW God wants you to do concerning your talent. Again, this does not have to be super deep or mysterious. It usually is that idea you can't get rid of, that thing you keep putting off, and so on. You know better than anyone what those things are.

The key is to WRITE IT DOWN!

4. Choose the one item you can take action on THIS WEEK!

Let's take baby steps here. Many times the reason we get paralyzed and don't move on what God reveals to us is that we try to take on the entire task. Take one step to reach the "low hanging fruit"; the task that's easiest to accomplish this week.

5. Choose the next creative goal that can be approached ...and complete it next week!

This is the reason why you need to write these down on something you can easily refer back to. You need to refer back to your goals so that you can not only stay on task but also celebrate what you complete. There's nothing better than seeing a goal list with items crossed out!

4 Steps to Open Doors for Your Art

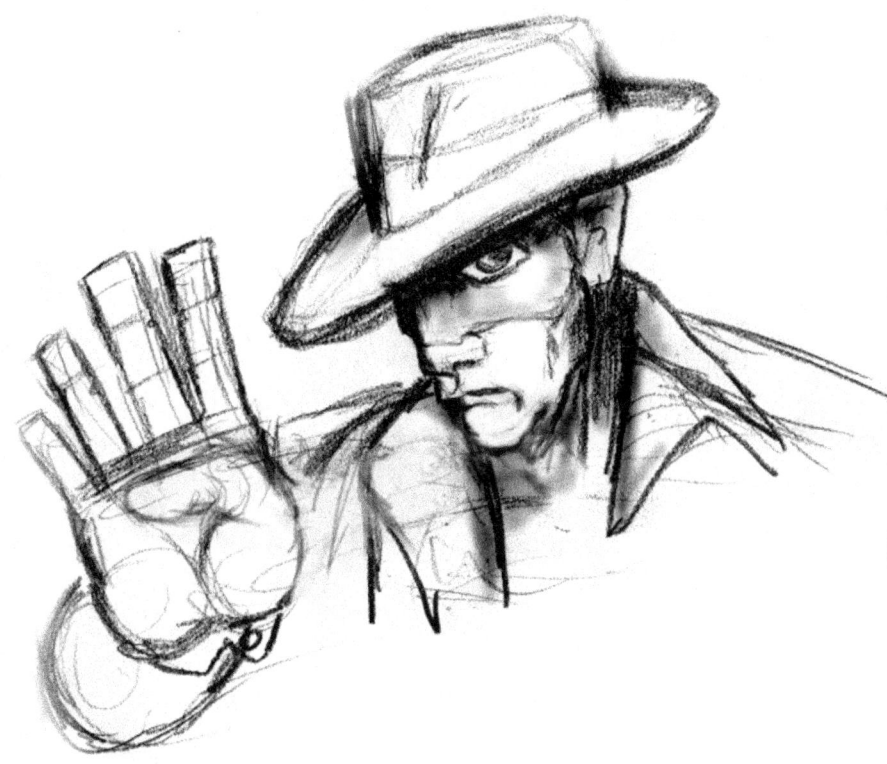

TIP NUMBER: 11

4 Steps to Open Doors for Your Art

Want to hear from God concerning your talent this week?

Sure you do! If you are serious, I challenge you to do these four simple steps:

Jeremiah 33:3 teaches us the following:
"Call to me and I will answer you and tell you great and unsearchable things you do not know."

Step 1: Call unto God and ask Him to show you what creative direction, step, or task He wants you take this week.

Step 2: Prayerfully watch for Him to open a door. Many times this will be subtle or unexpected. Often we are waiting for the parting of clouds and bolt of lightning with a chorus of angels in the background, but usually God speaks to us in a "still, small voice". Watch for the simple, the subtle, the unexpected:

"Then He said, "Go out, and stand on the mountain before the Lord." And behold, the Lord passed by, and a great and strong wind tore into the mountains and broke the rocks in pieces before the Lord, but the Lord was not in the wind; and after the wind an earthquake, but the Lord was not in the earthquake; and after the earthquake a fire, but the Lord was not in the fire; and after the fire a still small voice."
1 Kings 19:11-13

Step 3: As you sense God directing you, write it down! You can probably count the times you've sensed the Spirit of God directing you in the past already. How many of those instances have you failed to act on? Writing it down helps you to commit it to action.

Steps 4: I started not to include this one because I thought it was obvious (but God knows us so well!): Do It! Once He reveals it, follow through. Many times we pray and ask for God to give us direction. But we have yet to do the last thing He's already pointed out! So again, once God has revealed it, Do It!

3 Benefits to Artists & Designers Who Are Guided By God

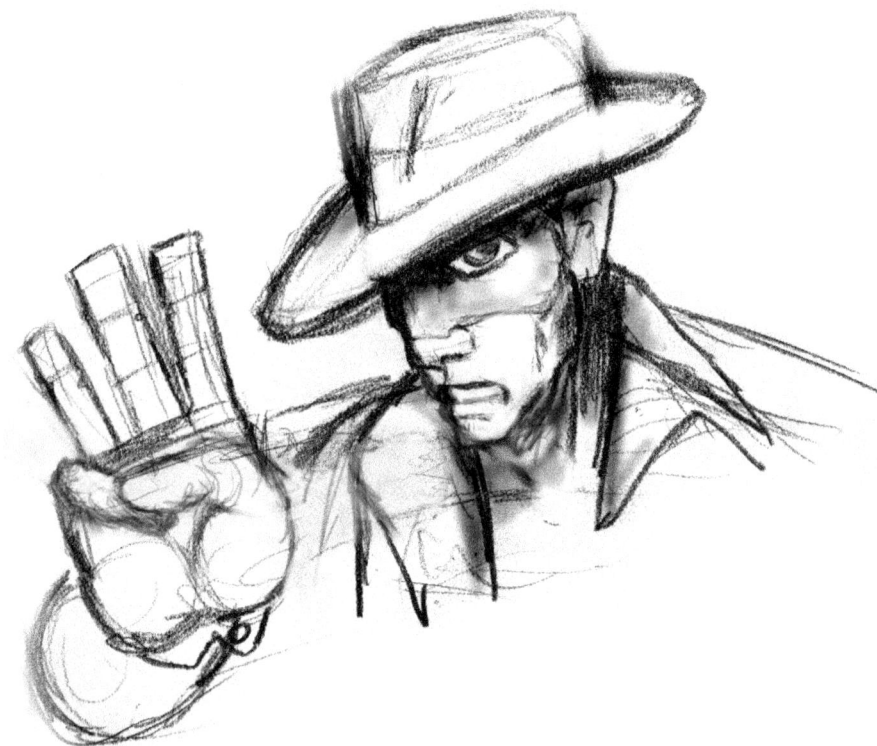

TIP NUMBER: 12

3 Benefits to Artists & Designers
Who Are Guided By God

This is actually Part 2 to an earlier topic where we determined that in order to become the artist who God actually daydreams and longs for you to become will require you to place your will in a position of Neutrality: a place where you set your ideas, opinions and passion down and be willing to go or do whatever God will have you to do.

Being neutral to your own idea positions you to be able to hear God's idea when He speaks. Your "voice" or will can be so loud that it actually drowns out the guiding voice of the Spirit of God, especially when it comes to your passion. Once you reach the willingness to go wherever God says "go", void of your own feelings about the matter, you will be able to hear His voice and receive His direction.

Here are the benefits of putting your will in neutral to God's direction:

1. A unique plan tailored just for YOU: God knows the plans He has for you. This includes the plans He has for you as an artist or designer. "For I know the plans I have for you," declares the LORD, "plans to prosper you and not to harm you, plans to give you hope and a future." Jeremiah 29:11 (New International Version)

2. Instruction and direction from His perspective: God will give you direction and insight based on what He knows is "coming around the corner." What we view is limited by our ability to only see "on the ground". God says in His Word "I will instruct thee and teach thee in the way which thou shalt go: I will guide thee with mine eye." Psalm 32:8

3. Secret or Insider information: God will give you secret and hidden information about your talent, opportunities, projects....and YOUR LIFE. "'Call to me and I will answer you and tell you great and unsearchable things you do not know." Jeremiah 33:3 (New International Version)

Be Sure to Visit
ArtLessonsFromGod.com

Everyone has asked these 3 questions:

Who am I?

Why am I here?

What should I be doing?

Art Lessons From God! is an online magazine published weekly by Kreative Kingdom, Inc. (a non-propfit organization). Our purpose is to help Artists and Designers discover their purpose by discussing those same questions from their point of view:

Who am I as an artist?

Why do I have this talent?

What does God want me to do with it?

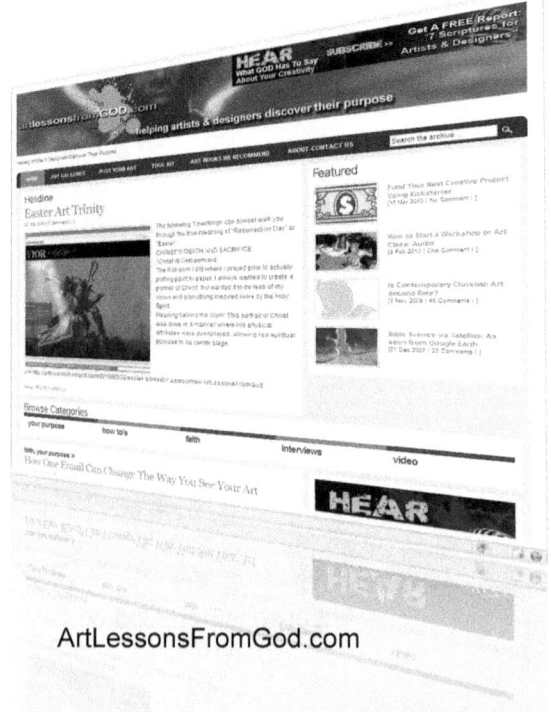

ArtLessonsFromGod.com

About The Author/Artist

Born in Portsmouth, VA, Tony Snipes has been drawing and painting nearly all of his life. He is trained in Graphic Design, Illustration, and Web Design and has worked in his craft within the corporate world and as a freelancer.

A few years ago, Tony discovered a deeper level of creativity when he realized there is a deeper relationship with God through Jesus Christ. Shortly after, he felt a desire to use his creative talents to glorify God. Tony believes that this is the key for any artist to discover their true purpose.

Tony resides in the beautiful foothills of South Carolina with his wife Monica and daughters Azsa, Anisa and Moriah.

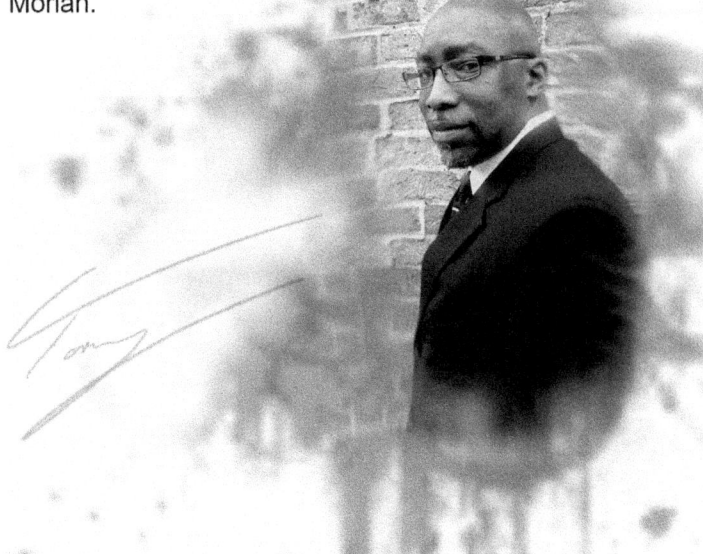